Those Big Bears

Jan Lee Wicker

Illustrations by Steve Weaver

Pineapple Press, Inc.
Sarasota, Florida

Photo Credits

Cover photo courtesy of Mike Carraway; Photos on pages 2, 26, 28 (inset), 32 (top), and 40 (with measuring tape) courtesy of David S. Maehr; Photos on pages 8, 18, and 46 courtesy of Jessie Williams, mediaforconservation.org; Photo on page 16 courtesy of Lee Wicker; Photos on pages 40 (bottom 2 claws), and 54 courtesy of Chris Wicker; Photo on page 30 by Jan Lee Wicker; Photos on pages 32 (bottom), 36 and 38 courtesy of Tom Gillespie; Photos on pages 20, and 28 (top) courtesy of Mike Carraway; Photos on pages 10, 12, 22, 24, 34, 42 courtesy of istock.com.

Inquiries should be addressed to:

Pineapple Press, Inc.
P.O. Box 3889
Sarasota, Florida 34230

www.pineapplepress.com

Library of Congress Cataloging-in-Publication Data
Wicker, Jan Lee,
Those big bears / Jan Lee Wicker ; illustrations by Steve Weaver.
p. cm.
Includes bibliographical references and index.
ISBN 978-1-56164-491-9 (hb : alk. paper)
ISBN 978-1-56164-492-6 (pb : alk. paper)
1. Bears--Juvenile literature. I. Weaver, Steve. II. Title.
QL737.C27W53 2011
599.78--dc22
2011004467

First Edition
Hb 10 9 8 7 6 5 4 3 2 1
Pb 10 9 8 7 6 5 4 3 2 1

Ages 6–9

Design by Steve Weaver
Printed in China

To my sister Teri Casey and my brother-in-law John, who
generously share their gift of hospitality

In memory of David Maehr, who was a friend
of the Florida panther and the American black bear.
His work helping wildlife continues on through
those whose lives he touched.

Contents

What is a bear?

A bear is a mammal with a large body and short legs. It has a long nose, a short tail, and shaggy hair. Bears live in many areas of the world. Most of them eat whatever plants and animals they can find. They usually live alone. Most of them take a very long sleep during the winter. Bears are good swimmers.

Is a giant panda a bear?

Yes. In the past scientists thought giant pandas were related to the raccoon family. The giant panda has one more bone on its front paw than other bears. The extra bone is opposite the other five fingers. This extra bone helps panda bears hold the bamboo they eat.

Is a koala a bear?

No. Many people call them "koala bears" because they look like teddy bears. Koalas and bears are both mammals. Even the smallest kind of bear is much bigger than a koala. Koalas have a pouch for their babies and bears do not. Baby bears are out on their own, but stay close to mother bear.

How many different kinds of bears are there?

There are eight different kinds of bears. The **black bear** is the most common. The **giant panda** is endangered. The **grizzly bear** is the best-known brown bear. The **sloth bear** has long hair on its ears. The **polar bear** is all white. The **spectacled bear** looks like it has on eyeglasses. The **Asiatic bear** is called the moon bear because of the moon-shaped mark on its chest. The **sun bear** has a mark on its chest that looks like a sun setting.

How big are bears?

Males are bigger than females. The smallest bear is the sun bear. It is about 4 feet long and weighs about 145 pounds. The next in size is the panda. The sloth, spectacled, Asiatic, and black bears are all around 6 feet long and weigh from 150 to 800 pounds. The grizzly bear can weigh 1,000 pounds and is about 9 feet long. The male polar bear is the biggest. It can stand over 10 feet tall and weighs over 1,400 pounds.

What do bears eat?

Most bears are omnivores. They eat grass, fish, berries, carrion (dead animals), small mammals, nuts, seeds, honey, and insects. The polar bear is a carnivore because it only eats meat. The panda eats mostly bamboo. Sloth bears have no front teeth. They suck up termites with their long tongue.

Can baby bears live by themselves?

No. A baby bear, called a cub, needs its mother for food and protection. A wildlife biologist may need to rescue bear cubs. This is the last resort because the cubs get used to being around humans. They may depend on people to care for them. Then it becomes hard for the cubs to be put back into the wild. This can be unsafe for people and the cubs.

How fast can polar bears swim?

Polar bears can swim faster than we can. They can swim 6 miles an hour. A polar bear can swim without stopping for 62 miles. It has skin between its toes (like a duck's webbed feet) to help it swim faster. When a polar bear dives under water, its nostrils close by themselves. We have to hold our nostrils closed. The polar bear can hold its breath for 2 minutes.

Why do bears stand on two legs?

Bears stand up on two legs for many reasons. If bears hear a noise, they stand up so they can see and smell the air better. Bears stand up to reach fruit in trees. They stand up to look scary. They will fight other bears on their hind legs. A bear will also stand up to scratch its back against a tree.

Why do bears climb trees?

Some bears climb trees to sleep up there. Black bears climb trees to get away from their enemies. A mother black bear will teach her cubs to climb a tree to be safe and to look for food. Grizzly bears are not good tree climbers. They have to stand and fight if their cubs are in danger.

What are bear cubs like?

Most bears have from one to three cubs at a time. Black bears can have as many as five. When bear cubs are born, their eyes are closed and they have very little fur. Cubs stay with their mothers for a year and a half. Panda cubs have all white hair when they are born. Their black hair comes in five days later.

Are all black bears black?

No. Most black bears are black, but not all of them. Some black bears are a reddish color, like the color of cinnamon. Others are brown and can be mistaken for a grizzly bear. Black bears can also be blond (yellow), blue-black, dark brown, or even white. White black bears are very rare.

What is the difference between a black bear and a grizzly bear?

The easiest way to tell them apart is the big shoulder hump of a grizzly bear. The profile of these two bears is also different. The face of a grizzly dips in between the eyes and the nose. The black bear has a straighter profile. Grizzly tracks show that their toes touch each other. The tracks of black bears show that there is space between their toes.

Why are panda bears endangered?

Giant pandas live in China in areas where they can find the bamboo that they eat. China now has over a billion people, so there is less room for pandas. Pandas have only one or two babies at a time. Scientists say there are less than 3,000 pandas left. Most now live in Chinese forest reserves and in zoos.

What good are bears?

Bears are an important part of the whole web of life. If bears are in the area, that means it is a good habitat for wildlife. Bears help to control the number of other animals in an area by eating the sick and injured animals. When bears eat, they move seeds around. Those seeds grow more plants for other animals to use. Many people spend lots of money to view and photograph bears. That is good for a community.

Autographed
Bear Photos

$1.00 each

Do bears play?

Yes. Mother bears play with cubs by wrestling with them. Bear cubs often play-fight with each other. This helps cubs get ready for when they will really fight. Bears also play by themselves. Black bears and pandas have been seen sliding down snow-covered hills all by themselves.

Black
Bear

Grizzly

Polar
Bear

How do bears use their claws?

Bears use their claws to dig up roots and small animals underground. Grizzly bears use their claws to dig their dens. Bears cut deep gashes into their enemies' skin when fighting. Bears' claws help them climb trees, dig insects out of logs, and knock beehives out of trees.

How do bears communicate?

All bears make noise. Some growl as a warning. But not all bears growl. A black bear might moan in fear, but it rarely growls. Bears may clack their teeth and blow if they are afraid. Bears can make a purring sound like a cat. They do this when they are nursing or really comfortable.

Where in the world do bears live?

Bears live all over the world except in Africa, Antarctica, and Australia. The polar bear lives around the North Pole. Black bears are found in North America. Brown bears live in North America, Europe, and Asia. Pandas, Asiatic bears, sloth bears,

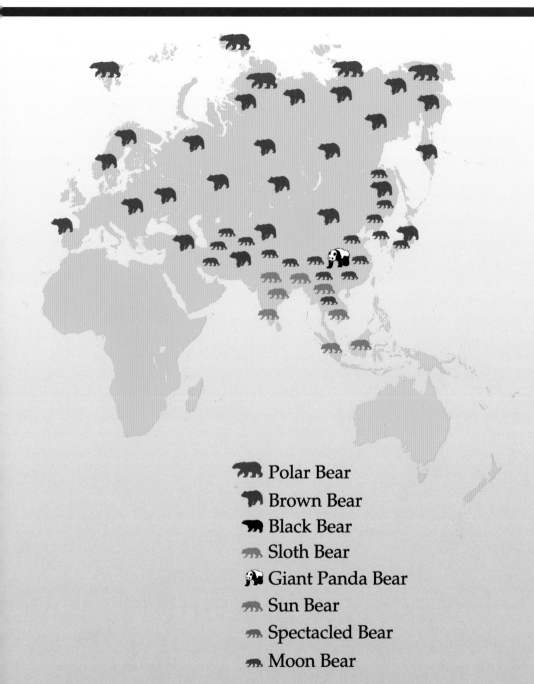

Polar Bear
Brown Bear
Black Bear
Sloth Bear
Giant Panda Bear
Sun Bear
Spectacled Bear
Moon Bear

and sun bears live in Asia. The only bear that lives in South America is the spectacled bear.

What do bears do in the winter?

Bears go to sleep when the weather is very cold. This is called hibernation. It isn't like when we go to sleep. Bears do not eat or eliminate waste for months at a time. Their body temperature can get as low as the outside temperature. The young bear in the photo is trying to wake up after a long winter sleep in his den.

Activities

Black Bear Paw Print

You will need:
    black tempera paint or black fabric paint
    white paper or light-colored T-shirt
    paintbrush
    fine-tip black magic marker or black fabric paint pen

Step #1:
Put a small amount of black paint into a flat dish.

Step #2:
Use your paintbrush and paint the side of your fist (without your pinky finger) to press onto the paper.

Step #3:
Press your painted fist sideways onto the paper.

Step #4:
Press your pointer finger into the paint and add five toes. Be sure to put space between the toes and space between the pad of the foot and the toes.

Step #5:
Add a black dot at the tip of each toe for the claw print.

Powdered Panda

You will need:
  2 small powdered donuts
  4 mini Tootsie Rolls
  4 chocolate morsels

Step #1:
Put one donut above the other so they touch. One is the head and one is the body.

Step #2:
Put one of the Tootsie Rolls on either side of the neck as arms.
Put the other two Tootsie Rolls on at the bottom of the body as legs.

Step #3:
Add two chocolate morsels as eyes on the top donut. Put the other two on top of the head as ears.

Polar Bear Claw

You will need:
  1 honey bun pastry
  vanilla frosting
  several slivered almonds
  plastic knife

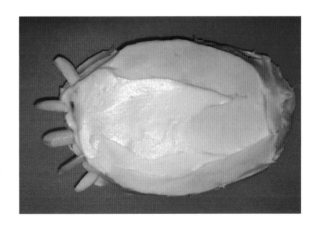

Step #1:
Hold on to the pastry as you push several slivered almonds into one of the longer ends of the pastry.

Step #2:
Using the knife, spread some icing on the top of the pastry.

Step #3:
Eat your bear claw! Yum! Yum!

Finger-paint a Grizzly

You will need:

finger-paint paper	scissors
brown washable finger-paint	hole puncher
black paper	white construction paper
black pen	bear trace pattern

Step #1:
Put enough finger-paint to spread over the paper with your hands until the paper is covered.

Step #2:
Using your fingernails, scratch back and forth in one direction until the paper is full of scratches. This is the hair of the grizzly bear.

Step #3:
Let the paint dry—hanging up if possible to make the paper remain flat. Trace the pattern of the bear onto the paper and cut it out.

Step #4:
Glue the bear's body, legs, and head on the piece of construction paper.

Step #5:
Punch out two black circles, one for the bear's eyeball and one for the nose. Add claws and teeth to finish your grizzly.

Where to Learn More about Bears

Books

Star, Fleur, and Lorrie Mack. *Watch Me Grow: Panda*. New York, NY: DK Publishing, 2008.

Bennett, Elizabeth. *Powerful Polar Bears*. New York, NY: Scholastic, Inc., 2007.

Morgan, Sally. *Animal Lives: Bears*. Laguna Hills, CA: QEB Publishing, 2005.

Helbrough, Emma. *Usborne Beginners: Bears*. New York, NY: Scholastic, Inc., 2002.

Feeney, Kathy. *Our Wild World: Black Bears*. Minnetonka, MN: NorthWord, 2000.

Websites

www.polarbearsinternational.org

www.pandasinternational.org

www.nationalzoo.si.edu

www.kids.nationalgeographic.com

www.usborne-quicklinks.com
(Type the keywords "beginners bears")

Glossary

bamboo – a hard type of grass that is hollow, grows as tall as trees, and is often used as a fishing pole

carnivore – any animal that eats other animals

carrion – dead animals

community – an area or neighborhood where people live and work

cub – the baby of a bear (or the baby of other animals such as lions, raccoons, and tigers)

den – a cave-type place where bears live (polar bears dig dens of ice)

endangered species – a group of animals (or plants) in danger of dying off so there would be no more of them in the world

habitat – a place where an animal (or plant) can be found

hibernate – to spend the winter in a kind of sleep where the body temperature, breathing, and heart rate are much lower than normal

marsupials – an animal whose newborn babies are carried by the female in a pouch in the front of her body (males don't have pouches)

omnivores – animals that eat both plants and animals

orphaned – when the parents die and no one is there to care for the young

profile – the side view of a person or animal's face

web of life – the connections between all living things

About the Author

Jan Lee Wicker has taught pre-kindergarten through first grade for the past 29 years. She loves to teach about animals and takes great joy in writing nonfiction for young children. She is pictured here with a life-size polar bear at FirstSafari in Moore County, NC. She and her husband Chris live in Roanoke Rapids, NC. They have two grown sons, a wonderful daughter-in-law, and their first grandchild, Hannah.

She has also written *Those Funny Flamingos, Those Delightful Dolphins, Those Excellent Eagles,* and *Those Magical Manatees.* You can visit her website at www.janleewicker.com.

Index

(Numbers in **bold** refer to photographs.)

Here are the other books in this series. For a complete catalog, visit our website at www.pineapplepress.com. Or write to Pineapple Press, P.O. Box 3889, Sarasota, Florida 34230-3889, or call (800) 746-3275.

Each title in the Those Amazing Animals series, written for children ages 6–9, has 20 questions and answers, 20 photos, and 20 illustrations by Steve Weaver.

Those Amazing Alligators by Kathy Feeney. Photographs by David M. Dennis. Discover the differences between alligators and crocodiles; learn what alligators eat, how they communicate, and much more.

Those Beautiful Butterflies by Sarah Cussen. This book answers 20 questions about butterflies— their behavior, why they look the way they do, how they communicate, and much more.

Those Colossal Cats by Marta Magellan. Twenty questions and answers about lions, tigers, leopards, and the other big cats.

Those Delightful Dolphins by Jan Lee Wicker. Learn the difference between a dolphin and a porpoise, find out how dolphins breathe and what they eat, and learn how smart they are and what they can do.

Those Excellent Eagles by Jan Lee Wicker. Photographs by H. G. Moore III. Learn all about those excellent eagles—what they eat, how fast they fly, why the American bald eagle is our nation's national bird.

Those Funny Flamingos by Jan Lee Wicker. Learn why those funny birds are pink, stand on one leg, eat upside down, and much more.

Those Lively Lizards by Marta Magellan. Photographs by James Gersing. In this book you'll meet lizards that can run on water, some with funny-looking eyes, some that change color, and some that look like little dinosaurs.

Those Magical Manatees by Jan Lee Wicker. Twenty questions and answers about manatees— you'll find out more about their behavior, why they're endangered, and what you can do to help.

Those Outrageous Owls by Laura Wyatt. Photographs by H. G. Moore III. Learn what owls eat, how they hunt, and why they look the way they do. You'll find out what an owlet looks like, why horned owls have horns, and much more.

Those Peculiar Pelicans by Sarah Cussen. Photographs by Roger Hammond. Find out how much food those peculiar pelicans can fit in their beaks, how they stay cool, and whether they really steal fish from fishermen.

Those Terrific Turtles by Sarah Cussen. Photographs by David M. Dennis. You'll learn the difference between a turtle and a tortoise, and find out why they have shells. Meet baby turtles and some very, very old ones, and even explore a pond.

Those Voracious Vultures by Marta Magellan. Photographs by James Gersing and Ron Magill. Learn all about vultures—the gross things they do, what they eat, whether a turkey vulture gobbles, and more.